Beaver Colony

Julie Murray

Abdo Kids Junior
is an Imprint of Abdo Kids
abdopublishing.com

Abdo
ANIMAL GROUPS
Kids

abdopublishing.com

Published by Abdo Kids, a division of ABDO, P.O. Box 398166, Minneapolis, Minnesota 55439.
Copyright © 2019 by Abdo Consulting Group, Inc. International copyrights reserved in all countries.
No part of this book may be reproduced in any form without written permission from the publisher.
Abdo Kids Junior™ is a trademark and logo of Abdo Kids.

Printed in the United States of America, North Mankato, Minnesota.

052018

092018

THIS BOOK CONTAINS
RECYCLED MATERIALS

Photo Credits: Alamy, Glow Images, iStock, Science Source, Shutterstock

Production Contributors: Teddy Borth, Jennie Forsberg, Grace Hansen

Design Contributors: Christina Doffing, Candice Keimig, Dorothy Toth

Library of Congress Control Number: 2017960607

Publisher's Cataloging-in-Publication Data

Names: Murray, Julie, author.

Title: Beaver colony / by Julie Murray.

Description: Minneapolis, Minnesota : Abdo Kids, 2019. | Series: Animal groups |
    Includes glossary, index and online resources (page 24).

Identifiers: ISBN 9781532107801 (lib.bdg.) | ISBN 9781532108785 (ebook) |
    ISBN 9781532109270 (Read-to-me ebook)

Subjects: LCSH: Beavers--Behavior--Juvenile literature. | Animal behavior--Juvenile literature. |
    Social behavior in animals--Juvenile literature. | Animal species--Juvenile literature.

Classification: DDC 599.37--dc23

Table of Contents

Beaver Colony

Beavers live in a family group.

It is called a colony.

It has 2 to 12 beavers in it.

They take care of each other.

They groom each other.

This keeps them clean.

They work together.

They chew down trees.

They build a dam. This stops
the water flow.

They build a lodge. This is where they live.

A bear is near! They slap their tails.

This warns the others.

They swim to safety!

Being in a Colony

2 to 12 in a colony

build a dam together

build a lodge together

groom each other

Glossary

dam
built by beavers in flowing water to create ponds as protection against predators.

lodge
a dome-shaped beaver home built out of branches and mud with entrances under and above water.

Index

Visit **abdokids.com** and use this code to access crafts, games, videos, and more!

Abdo Kids Code:
ABK7801